1 MONTH OF
FREE
READING

at

www.ForgottenBooks.com

By purchasing this book you are eligible for one month membership to ForgottenBooks.com, giving you unlimited access to our entire collection of over 1,000,000 titles via our web site and mobile apps.

To claim your free month visit:

www.forgottenbooks.com/free660266

ISBN 978-0-484-29589-5
PIBN 10660266

total, 916. Miscellaneous—table cloths, 36; umbrellas, 48; bibles, 102; watches, 204; rings, 216; Waterloo medals, 48—total, 654:— sum total, 6,195. If we divide the 1,381,200 of such pledges in Edinburgh, we will find that each place effects as near as possible 41,000 annually, or 3,500 monthly. But some of these establishments transact an almost incredible amount of business. I have it on the best authority that one office in a poor district, betwixt the Castle and Holyrood, effected in one month 11,000 pledges! All the 11,000 were low pledges, sums below 10s, with the exception of 30, which were high pledges, above 10s. This surely reveals a social condition among the poor of Edinburgh that needs very special attention and treatment. I have had the most harrowing interviews with working men, almost driven to despair and madness about their families, in consequence of wives pawning, with ruinous facility, everything during their absence at work. One man told me that his house was stripped of everything, his daughters were unable to cross the door—their mother having stolen and pledged their things while they slept, and that unredeemed pledges were lying in the house in 'goupons!' I have seen strong men literally broken down with grief and starvation, large wages being consumed by pawnbrokers and publicans. Allow me, also, to give you a brief narrative of other authentic cases—a mere sample of hundreds more—from the private diary of a gentleman whose extensive intercourse with the poor gives weight to his words. A working man, earning all the year round 18s per week, has a wife and children. His wife is given to intemperance, and takes fearful rounds of drinking. He does everything in his power to keep her from getting drink—keeps the money and means out of her way— pays all the accounts himself, and does everything he can to prevent her drinking; but all utterly fails on account of the facility given to such characters by the pawnshops. I have known her three or four times strip the children and herself of clothes, leaving just rags enough to cover them, and empty the house of everything she could carry away—the bed clothes, the clock, and pictures from the wall— the very pots and pans; and when all such things are gone, in desperation she breaks open every lock in the house, and leaves nothing. I have known her poor husband, week after week, have to take the shirt from his back, wash and dry it on Sabbath, that he might have it clean to go to his work on Monday. When all in the house is gone, then she goes to the clubman, gets £1 or £2 worth of cloth in her husband's name, with the promise to pay it at so much a week. Of course her husband never sees it, it goes straight to the pawnshop; and the first notice that he gets of it is months after, when his wages are arrested for the payment of it. The husband is kept from church, the children are kept from school —they have to sleep without bed-clothes, and live almost without body-clothes; and for all this the pawnshop is much to blame."

All this is going on with aggravations to the present hour.

THE BRITISH ARMY

IN

1868.

BY

SIR CHARLES E. TREVELYAN, K.C.B.

LONDON:
LONGMANS, GREEN, AND CO.
1868.

LONDON: PRINTED BY
SPOTTISWOODE AND CO., NEW-STREET SQUARE
AND PARLIAMENT STREET

PREFACE.

THE first part of this pamphlet is a summary, carefully revised up to the present date, of the proposals originally made by me to the Purchase Commission in 1857, and brought forward a second time in the beginning of last year. The last part deals with the remainder of the subject which had not previously been treated by me, and especially with the fundamental questions of the term of the soldier's service and the constitution of the army of reserve.

It has been my aim to make this last part a just statement of the result of the ample discussion which this branch of the subject has lately undergone; and there are few of the able writers who have helped to form a sound public opinion upon it who will not recognise some of their proposals built into the system which I have ventured to recommend. I wish more particularly to acknowledge my obligations to Major General Riddell, C.B., R.A.; Lieut.-Col. Acland, M.P., Devon Rifle Volunteers; Colonel Adair, Suffolk Militia Artillery, A.D.C. to the Queen; Colonel A. C. Robertson, Major Bannatyne, Lieut.-Col. Reilly, R.A., Major Leahy, R.E., Captain Phipps, R.A., Major J. Bevan-Edwards, R.E., Lieut.-Col. G. Ashley Maude,

C.B., R.A., and two other military writers who have given no clue to their names. So much, however, is apparent, that the reform of the army is chiefly proceeding, as it ought to do, from the only two corps which have as yet had the advantage of a thorough professional education.

If my labours on this subject should be productive of any public benefit, it will be chiefly due to the extremely kind and never-failing assistance I have received, since I was first called upon to give my evidence before the Purchase Commission, from one of my oldest and best friends, Colonel Haliday, now Commandant and Inspector-General of Musketry. It has been my practice to submit all my proposals to his criticism before finally adopting them; and a more experienced and judicious adviser it would have been impossible to have.

The order in which the different parts of the subject are treated is:—

THE

BRITISH ARMY IN 1868.

LORD BACON remarks, in his 'Regimen of Health'—
'Beware of any sudden change in any point of diet,
and if necessity enforce it, fit the rest to it; for it is
a secret both in nature and in State, that it is safer to
change many things than one.' The practical wisdom
of this maxim deserves the attention of those who
object to army-reform because the proposed new
state of things is inconsistent with some of the conditions belonging to an existing old one.

I.

HOW TO MAKE OUR ARMY IN A TRUE SENSE POPULAR, AND, AS REGARDS RECRUITING SELF-SUPPORTING.

The armies which laid the foundation of our military
reputation at Crecy, Poitiers and Agincourt, included
a middle-class element in the yeomen-archers, to
whom those victories were chiefly due. The army
which secured the liberty of England and conquered
Ireland and Scotland, was eminently a middle-class

army. Upon this followed a great reaction, under the influence of which our military system was re-moulded in the form which it retains to this day. The model adopted was the strictest type of the feudal system. The preux chevalier was translated into 'officer and gentleman,' and the humble retainer became the 'common soldier,' while the inter-mediate classes had no place whatever allotted to them. The feudal prejudices, which have yielded everywhere else to the feelings induced by a happier state of society, survive in full force in the army. Between the officer and the private a great gulf is fixed.* The distinction is essentially one of caste.

* In the programme of a lecture recently delivered at the United Service Institution by a regimental commanding officer, on 'The Appoint-ment and Promotion of Regimental Officers,' it was laid down as a primary condition, 'That there should be a great difference between the social position of the officers and privates of the army.' Contrast with this the following description of the relative position of the officers and men of the French army, extracted from the *Moniteur du Soir* of the 5th March last:—

'Chez nous, les cadres sont homogènes du premier échelon de la hiér-archie jusqu'au dernier. Du caporal au maréchal de France les grades vont se succédant, sans démarcation infranchissable; d'un degré à l'autre, point de brusque enjambement, de grands sauts à franchir. Le sergent-major échange facilement ses galons d'or contre l'épaulette de sous-lieu-tenant, et même il est un grade intermédiaire, celui d'adjudant, qui donne droit au port de l'épaulette, et dont les titulaires, pourtant, ne sont que sous-officiers.

'C'est un lien entre deux catégories de grades.

'Plus haut, le capitaine n'est pas très-loin du commandant, et enfin un colonel est bien près d'un général.

'Il en résulte une entente admirable entre tous les grades, une sou-plesse extrême dans le jeu du service, une émulation très-vive et très-précieuse; enfin pour les grades inférieurs, ces liens honorables qui les rattachent de si près aux grades supérieurs, inspirent à ceux qui les occu-pent une fierté légitime et un fier sentiment de dignité.

'Chez nous, les sous-officiers sont aux sept dixièmes officiers, selon l'heureuse expression du général Ambert. Entre eux et leurs officiers

It is true that many young men of the middle class enter the army, but they are incorporated at once into the upper stratum as officers. They chiefly belong to the new families created by our industrial system, and their object is to take rank officially as 'gentlemen.' It is also true that a few exceptional promotions are made of non-commissioned officers, but these only receive a good-natured toleration, and their uncomfortable position illustrates the present utter want of harmonious relation between the status of the officers and men of the army.

The object to be aimed at is to make the army a true representation of the nation. It should be neither more aristocratic nor more democratic than the rest of English society. The upper, the middle and the lower classes cordially co-operate in every other public and private undertaking, and why should the army be the solitary exception? Since the beginning of the century the middle class has enormously developed; the present flourishing state of the country is chiefly owing to their exertions; and they have twice within the same period shown,

existe une familiarité respectueuse, déférente et reconnaissante, sans envie chez les premiers, affable, paternelle et pleine de sollicitude chez les derniers; et cette familiarité, qui produit sur le champ de bataille et dans les cas difficiles des miracles de dévouement, ne nuit en rien à la discipline; dans le service et dans le rang, l'obéissance est absolue.

'Enfin, chez nous, la croix d'honneur qui brille sur les uniformes les plus modestes est un trait d'union entre tous: c'est l'égalité devant la gloire.

'Enfin, l'avancement chez nous est ouvert à tous, et l'on compte plusieurs maréchaux de France qui ont tiré leur bâton de commandement du fond de leur giberne de soldat.

'Nombreux sont les généraux qui ont porté le havre-sac.'

by voluntarily organising for the national defence, that they do not yield to any portion of the community in military spirit and capacity. When this class, taken in its widest sense, shall be included, our army will come up to the full standard of the strength, the intelligence, and the moral qualities of our population; and, from being in its plan and design a purely aristocratic institution, the British army will become emphatically a popular army, and our recruiting difficulties will be at an end.

In the rest of Europe this object is secured by compulsory conscription, but it may be still more perfectly attained by voluntary enlistment. The voluntary principle is based upon the craving of mankind to improve their condition; and, if the army were properly regulated, abundant means exist of gratifying this natural desire without creating a single new appointment or making any further addition to the pay of the soldier. While in other lines of life the rewards have been increasing, and it has become easier to rise to fortune and distinction, the monopoly of office in the army has remained as close as ever. A change for the worse has consequently taken place in the class of men who enter the ranks, and for some years past there has been an increasing difficulty in finding among them men qualified to be non-commissioned officers.

An indispensable preliminary to all improvement is to abolish purchase, and to increase the pay of officers of every rank sufficiently to enable them to live upon it in a suitable manner. The State might then reasonably require that no person should receive a commission who had not prepared himself to enter at once on the effective discharge of his duties.

In every well-constituted army there are only two modes of admission to the rank of officer, based upon two different kinds of experience.

The first of these is through a military college, which answers the double purpose of weeding out the incompetent and ill-conducted, and of teaching the rudiments of military science. The entrance to the college should be by competition, and the cost should be entirely defrayed by the parents, who might fairly be expected to spend, in completing the general and professional education of their sons, a portion of the sums now paid by them for commissions.

The other mode of admission is promotion from the ranks. This offers two great advantages. Every candidate must have acquired practical knowledge of the duties of privates and non-commissioned officers, and of their ways of thinking and feeling, before he can be placed in a position of command; and his character and capacity must be so completely known to his superior officers, that there can be no mistake as to his fitness. Commissions should be given on the ground of fitness only, claims on other grounds being otherwise rewarded, so that young men who possess qualifications for the military profession, may hope to be promoted to a commission after a short period of service. Necessary educational attainments should be tested by examination, and proper means of instructing the junior officers and men in military, administrative, and sanitary science should be provided by the improvement of the regimental schools, and by the appointment to each regiment of a captain-instructor who has passed at the staff college, as recommended by the late Sir Thomas Franks and by Sir William Mansfield. What follows is from Sir Thomas Franks' examination before the Purchase Commission :—

' 3342. What opportunities has an officer in the English army of acquiring any knowledge of his profession except purely regimental knowledge ?—I do not think they have opportunities sufficient; there ought to be in each regiment a captain or sub-altern capable of assisting the junior officers, if so inclined, in their professional studies. He might also superintend, with great advantage to the non-commissioned officers and privates, the regimental adult schools; but for this he should, of course, receive extra pay from the Government. Such is, I believe, the system in the French and Prussian armies.'

Sir William Mansfield wrote as follows in a letter to myself :—

' The Staff College would furnish captain-instructors for regiments.

' The duties of such functionaries should by no means be confined to the mere supervision of the cadets. They would, of course, take charge of the regimental schools, both of adults and children, with the regulated staff of schoolmasters, &c. &c.

' The lectures they would give, and their practical instruction in surveying, and so forth, would be open to the more advanced of the men, as well as to all the officers, and would enable those of the former who chose to qualify, to aspire, under certain conditions, to direct commissions, or to be admitted to the class of cadets. It would be their business also to assist young officers studying for the Staff College.

' I attribute an immense importance to this suggestion—viz. affording the means in the regiment of instruction, lectures, &c., to the young officers and the men. At present the public scolds the officers for wasting their time. But no practical means and stimulus are afforded them, and the soldiers stand greatly in need of a more official recognition of their studies and of larger encouragement than can be given by the non-commissioned schoolmaster.

'In short, the institution I contemplate would, I think, be the binding medium of the system you propose, and finally weld in one mass the officers and men, and thereby *democratise* the army. By this I mean inviting the people to the army according to broad principles of utility, and the motives by which men of all classes are induced to choose their lines of life. This I conceive to be the object of your proposals. I am sure that until it is effected by some means or other, we shall go on patching at our old, worn-out, and, in a certain sense, discreditable institutions, without getting at the heart of the nation for military purposes.'

In the Austrian, Prussian, and Russian armies, cadets ('aspirants,' or, as they are called in Prussia, 'volunteers,') perform all the duties of privates, and are promoted in the ordinary way to be non-commissioned officers, before they become eligible for commissions. In the French army there are no cadets, but the best of the non-commissioned officers are promoted to commissions. Of these two arrangements, the French is to be preferred, because, by opening the military career to the whole nation, it offers a strong inducement to a superior class of men to enlist, and extends the choice of officers to the whole army, instead of confining it to a few young men who had previously been appointed cadets. In practice, however, the two plans would have a great deal in common, for as soon as an assured prospect appeared of obtaining a commission through the ranks, young men of fair education, force and activity of character, and decided military tastes, but with no aptitude for the examinations and course of study at a military college (such young men abound in the militia and volunteers), would enlist expressly with a view to the higher promotion, and would associate, as comrades, with each other and with the best and most intelligent of the privates who enlisted from the ordinary motives, until they were promoted to be non-commissioned officers.

In order to give such reasonable prospect of promotion, contingent upon qualification and character, as would attract well-educated young men into the service, and influence their conduct when they are in it, and to prevent the door of promotion, which is opened wide in times of need like the Peninsular and Crimean wars, from being again shut when the exigency has passed, a fixed proportion of the commissions falling vacant in each regiment should be assigned to the non-commissioned officers, *provided a sufficient number of qualified candidates of that rank are forthcoming.* In his examination before the Recruiting Commission of 1859–60, his Royal Highness the Commander-in-Chief three times expressed his opinion (Questions 5267–8) that there could be no objection to this arrangement.*

* Question 5267. A number of commissions are given to persons from the ranks. Is it the opinion of your Royal Highness that if a certain proportion of all the death vacancies were so given, it would be an inducement to recruiting? At present a great number are given, but there is not a definite proportion?—*There would be no harm in that.* There is a difficulty in making it definite, because it must depend so much upon the number of vacancies. Of latter years the vacancies without purchase have been very large, and the consequence has been that we have given a great many more than usual to the non-commissioned officers. In years of peace the numbers are very limited, and we must apportion a

The reorganisation of the civil departments of the army now in progress, is based upon the principle of selecting the members of the administrative corps from the officers, non-commissioned officers, and privates of the army. This will give nearly five hundred civil appointments of a kind peculiarly suited to our industrial middle class.

After these arrangements have been made, the army may be accepted by all classes of our population as a national establishment in which they have a new and peculiar interest, because, whether they have a turn for business or for a purely military life, they will find in it a corresponding career, with liberal rewards to encourage them.

II.

RETIREMENT AND PROMOTION.

It is, I believe, generally admitted that the regimental ranks should be confined to four—lieutenant, captain, lieutenant-colonel, and colonel; the ensigns becoming lieutenants, the majors lieutenant-colonels,

certain number for the cadets at Sandhurst. Of course we divide the others among the non-commissioned officers and that reserved list which I have for commissions without purchase, which is very limited. Therefore it must be a give-and-take arrangement, and I do not exactly see how you could lay down any very specific proportion. *You might lay down a proportion to the number of vacancies; there can be no objection to that;* but I do not think that it would increase the recruiting, because I think the soldiers are now convinced that whenever they have a good claim it will always be considered; I think that there is that feeling throughout the service. Question 5268. The suggestion is not as regards soldiers, but to induce persons to enter who do not know the rule?—*I see no objection to that arrangement.*

and the lieutenant-colonels commanding regiments colonels. But, although the two ranks of field-officers would be included in the regimental establishments, they should be *army* ranks. In other words, the colonels, lieutenant-colonels, and captains should be placed, in order of seniority, on general lists; and the promotion to the lieutenant-colonelcies should be made from the whole of the captains belonging to the same branch of the army who have served a certain fixed time, and the colonels should, in like manner, be promoted from the lieutenant-colonels. One of the advantages of making the field ranks army ranks is, that officers may then be posted, on their promotion, either to their former or to new regiments, as circumstances may render desirable. It is often expedient that an officer should commence his career as a field-officer in a different regiment from the comrades with whom he has associated familiarly as lieutenant and captain, and this is especially the case when his promotion has not been according to seniority.* If these changes were made, the other branches of the army would be assimilated to the Artillery and Engineers so far as regards the number and designation of the ranks and the making of the promotions on general lists down to the rank of captain. The difference that would remain would be, that there would be an element of selection in making the promotions in the other branches of the

---

* The objections which formerly existed to transferring field officers from one regiment to another have been much diminished by the increased facilities of communication, and by the much smaller proportion of the army now stationed in the colonies.

army instead of the pure seniority of the scientific corps ; and the plan of promoting on general lists would stop at the promotion from captain to lieutenant-colonel, instead of going a step further down. I am aware that in theory the Artillery and Engineers are regiments, but they have long since outgrown the regimental character and must now be considered as separate branches of the army.

There is a fixed establishment of 272 general officers, of whom 150 receive stipends varying from £1,000 to £2,200 as titular colonels of regiments, and the remainder are paid at the uniform rate of £455 5s. a year. There is a striking inconsistency in these scales of remuneration, and the smaller of the two is a poor reward for officers who have given their entire service to the public, besides having paid heavily for their steps. They cannot live upon it in a manner suited to their rank if they have not also private means. As a prospective arrangement, the aggregate fund should be redistributed in stipends suited to the respective grades of major-general, lieutenant-general, general, and field-marshal. General officers would then be paid only as such, and the nominal rank of regimental colonel would merge in that of the colonel actually commanding the regiment.

As the State will now have to provide suitable means of retirement for officers of every grade, it has become necessary to determine what rules should be laid down with this object in the ranks below that of major-general. Considerable progress has been made in the solution of this question by the excellent report of Mr. Childers' Committee on the system of retirement in the Artillery and Engineers; and what we have to consider is, how far the proposals of the Committee must be modified to make them equally applicable to every branch of the army.

The indispensable conditions of military efficiency are physical activity in the lower, and intellectual ability in the higher ranks. The rules of retirement ought, therefore, to be so framed as to secure the highest possible average of these qualifications. This is a case in which we cannot act by individual selection. All that can be done is to lay down such rules as will operate in the direction desired, and secure a general result in our favour.

The circumstances of military service, especially in the British army, which has so large a share of foreign service, are not favourable to married life; and they become less so as children increase, and their education has to be provided for. Besides this, as officers advance in age, their bodily energies flag; they feel more and more inclined towards a settled home, with all its comforts and advantages; and they have to consider whether their personal tastes, their attainments, their professional reputation, their prospect of being selected for the higher honours and rewards, make it expedient for them finally to cast in their lot with the army. The inducements to retire should be brought to bear upon the period when these motives are at their maximum. This is required in the interest both of public economy and of the officers themselves. The current will be more rapid if the sluice is opened where the waters are already prepared to flow; and as the expense of maintaining the necessary circulation will under any circumstances be heavy, our resources ought to be made to go as far as possible. The practical question, therefore, is in what manner pensions should be adjusted to length of service.

Officers were formerly allowed to retire on permanent half-pay after twenty-one years' service; but since 1861 the qualifying period has been extended to twenty-five years. After thirty years' service, officers are eligible to retire on full pay.

The scale recommended by Mr. Childers' Committee for the Artillery and Engineers, is as follows:—

Number of Years' Service	Annuity	Probable Age	Probable Value of Annuity
22	£ 250 increasing by £25 annually to	42	£ 3,270
25	325	45	4,080
28	400	48	4,780
30	450 increasing by £15 annually to	50	5,050
35	525	55	5,400
40	600	60	5,510

I am inclined to think that the existing rule furnishes the sounder basis, and that Mr. Childers' scale would be improved if it were confined to its three middle terms—that is, from twenty-five to thirty years' service, with an intermediate advance at twenty-eight years. Taking the average of military officers, their general efficiency, even for regimental and ordinary staff purposes, goes on increasing until they are at least forty-five years of age. Numerous retirements will always take place at an earlier age—partly of young men of fortune, who only intend to pass a few years pleasantly and profitably in the army, and partly of those who, having acquired experience and reputation in the military profession, are tempted out of it by offers of public or private employment—but the State cannot be expected to make any sacrifice to induce its officers to resign at the most valuable period of their service, before they have rendered a full return for the training they have received. The object is the promotion of junior officers in regular succession; and this may be more equably and constantly attained, and in a manner more conducive to a high standard of efficiency, by the retirement of seniors than by the occasional elimination of a junior. These principles have been successfully applied to the Civil Service. The circumstances there are such that the period of discretionary retirement can be postponed to sixty years of age, previously to which no pension is allowed except for ill-health.

Assuming that the officers of the army will be recruited partly from young men who, after having received a liberal general education, will learn the rudiments of their profession at a military college, and partly from non-commissioned officers specially selected at any period of their service for their fitness to bear Her Majesty's commission, the time spent at a military college or in the ranks of the army should be allowed as part of the qualifying period for pension.

The interval of five years between 25 and 30 years' service would give officers ample time to consider whether they would retire from the service or follow it to the end. This alternative ought to be presented to them in the most explicit manner. Any prospective increase of pension would defeat the object of the whole arrangement, by bribing officers to remain whose retirement was demanded by the interests of the public service, of the officers below them, and, in a majority of cases, of the officers themselves. Mr. Childers' Committee was aware of the importance of this consideration, for they remarked that the pension

should be so graduated as to give an officer, after thirty years' service, little or no inducement to remain in the corps solely on account of any prospect of better retirement at a greater age. At fifty, an officer should practically have to make his election between seeking the higher commands in the corps, or (if his qualifications or circumstances unfit him for them) retiring from the service;

but the practice of the Committee was inconsistent with their principle, for they proposed to continue the graduated increase of pension up to forty years' service or sixty years of age. It is true that the annual increment of pension recommended by the Committee drops after thirty years' service from £25 to £15; but, if it really be desirable that officers should at fifty years of age have to elect between seeking the higher commands or retiring from the army, without being induced to remain by ' any prospect of better retirement at a greater age,' why is that prospect proposed to be held out to them?

. I shall not enter on the question of rates of pension, because they cannot be determined until the rates of pay have been settled. When appointment and promotion by purchase, and retirement by sale shall be abolished, the present complex and inadequate 'pay and allowances' must give place to consolidated rates adjusted on the principle of enabling officers of every rank to live in a suitable manner on their pay.

The policy of offering special facilities for commuting pensions for immediate payments is open to much doubt. The permanent interest of the State is on the side of paying pensions rather than on that of giving their equivalents in capital sums. The commutation of soldiers' pensions to enable them to settle in Canada ended in utter failure; and it would be scarcely less damaging to the credit and popularity of the service if there were frequent instances of old officers reduced to penury by the failure of the speculations for the sake of which they had sold their pensions. Officers can always raise money on their pensions at the market rates, and anything beyond this would be a bonus given to officers, at the expense of the public, to induce them to take their retired allowances in the shape of single lump sums. This case has nothing in common with that of the sums received by officers for the sale of their commissions, the transaction there being the recovery from other private individuals of a previous actual outlay.

· The Committee recognise the principle that there should be 'a limit of age for compulsory retirement from active duties,' but they only propose that every colonel should be placed on a reserved list at the age of sixty. The principle is, however, at least as applicable to the lower as to the higher ranks; and an age ought to be fixed in reference to each rank at which officers should retire as a matter of course, unless, for some special reason, the Commander-in-Chief should require their services for a further period.

With these modifications the system of retirement recommended by Mr. Childers' Committee should, I think, be applied to every branch of the army; and, whatever the cost of it may be, the nation may feel assured that its military service could not be efficiently maintained on more economical conditions.

The difficulties which have beset the subject of promotion have chiefly arisen from the inequalities which have been the consequence of a lax system. But it is now proposed that, previously to receiving their commissions, all candidates should be tested and brought up to a good standard, either by a course of professional instruction in a military college or by actual service in the ranks; and it will therefore only be necessary, in making promotions, to deal with cases of marked divergence.

Regimental seniority may safely be adopted as the rule of promotion from lieutenant to captain,* with

---

* Promotion is one of several points of view in which our military system will be rendered more manageable, by merging the rank of ensign in that of lieutenant, and the rank of major in that of lieutenant-colonel. This was noticed in Colonel Robertson's lecture at the United Service Institution on the system of promotion to be substituted for purchase, in which the use that might be made of specific qualifications as tests of fitness for promotion was pointed out.

an exception against misconduct and incompetency, and in favour of eminent merit.

The next step would be from captain to lieutenant-colonel. This is the 'strait gate' of the army, because the lowest rank of field officers is to the highest rank of company officers in the proportion of one to six. It is essential that field officers should be selected from the rank of captain with reference to their fitness for the command of a regiment. No new test is necessary for this purpose. Officers who have been for some time in command of a company or troop have passed their noviciate, and their character and qualifications are perfectly well known to their military superiors. The extracts given below from the chapters of the Queen's Regulations, entitled ' Half-yearly Inspections and Confidential Reports,' and ' Interior Economy of Corps,'* show that if the existing system is properly acted upon, those who may be periodically

---

* '189. PREPARATION OF CONFIDENTIAL REPORTS.—*The queries in the confidential reports are of so precise a nature as to require few detailed directions for filling them up.* The following general instructions, it is considered, will be sufficient for the purpose, and inspecting General officers are enjoined to be guided by and to act up to them :—

' *a. They should not be satisfied with brief replies in the negative or affirmative; reports so drawn up do not furnish the Commander-in-Chief with those particulars relating to the officers of a regiment which should enable him with due discrimination to benefit the meritorious or to note the undeserving.*

' *b.* It is not sufficient to state that a commanding officer has zeal, or that he maintains a well-regulated discipline; zeal may be unaccompanied by talent for command, and the system of discipline may have been established by others.

' *c. Amongst the field officers and captains there must be some superior to others, and they should be specially brought to notice, and not all be classed in the same category.*

' *d.* All questions of importance should be specially and decidedly reappointed to report on the promotions will have ample materials for the formation of a safe opinion. Even

ported upon in a manner that shall place the Commander-in-Chief in full possession of the actual state of a regiment as regards all ranks ; and this can only be effected by General officers entering into detail, and giving their answers fully, fearlessly, and conscientiously on every matter brought to their notice, or coming under their actual observation, whether it be one requiring praise or censure.

'190. TESTING OF CAPTAINS AND SUBALTERNS IN DRILL.—On the inspection of corps the General officer is to call upon one or more of the captains and subaltern officers—provided the latter shall have been doing duty for a reasonable period with the corps—*the former to put the regiment, and the latter a troop, battery, or company, through their exercise, field movements, and evolutions* ; such captains and subalterns to be selected indifferently and without previous notice given to them or to the commanding officer, *in order that it may be ascertained whether due attention has been shown to the instruction of every officer ; whether opportunities have been afforded to them of becoming acquainted with every part of their duty, and whether they have availed themselves of such opportunities.*

'191. MUSKETRY INSTRUCTION TO BE ATTENDED TO.—General officers are to give their special attention to the musketry instruction of the troops under their command, and are to be accompanied at their inspection, when practicable, by the District Inspectors of Musketry, for the purposes referred to in Part III. pars. 27 and 28 of the Musketry Regulations, 1867. When the General officer is not so accompanied, the cause is to be explained in the Confidential report.

'192. ALL AVAILABLE MEN TO ATTEND INSPECTIONS.—Care should be taken that every officer, non-commissioned officer, and man whose absence from parade is not absolutely indispensable, be required to attend at half-yearly inspections, in order that it may be satisfactorily shown that the military efficiency of all ranks is properly maintained.

'267. CONDUCT OF OFFICERS TO BE REPORTED IN CERTAIN CASES. —*It is the duty of a commanding officer to bring especially to the notice of the inspecting general without favour or partiality any officers who may be distinguished for attention to, and proficiency in, their duties ; as well as those who, from incapacity or habitual inattention, are deficient in a knowledge of their duties, or who show an indisposition to afford the commanding officer that support which he has a right to expect from them ; or who conduct themselves in a manner injurious to the efficiency and the credit of the corps. The penalties attached to such misconduct and neglect or ignorance of duty, will be* SUSPENSION OF PROMOTION *until a further report shall declare the officer to have proved himself equal to the performance of his duties, and free from any cause of censure : and removal from the service in the event of continued incapacity or negligence.*'

so, however, every officer's claim should be *considered* in the order of his seniority upon the list of captains of his branch of the army, and the promotion of those officers should be postponed whose fitness for the rank of field officer is open to reasonable doubt. It would, after all, be only the ' power of the veto ' which His Royal Highness the Commander-in-Chief told the Purchase Commission was ' much more easy to exercise than the power of selection.' Fitness for the command of a regiment is such a well-marked qualification that some captains would never pass the ordeal, and would remain with their regiments until they either voluntarily retired or got beyond the age at which they could serve in that rank.

If the promotions from captain to lieutenant-colonel are faithfully made on recorded public grounds, there will be no difficulty about those from lieutenant-colonel to colonel, or from colonel to major-general. Seniority should be observed as a general rule, to be departed from only in case of proved incompetency or misconduct on one hand, or superior ability or good service on the other; the invariable principle being that no officer should be promoted to a position of higher command who has not exhibited unmistakeable qualifications for it.

III.

PROBABLE AMOUNT OF THE COMPENSATION FOR THE ABOLI-
TION OF PURCHASE, AND OF THE CURRENT CHARGE OF
THE ARMY UNDER THE REVISED SYSTEM.

Besides the ordinary motives for compensating those who might otherwise suffer from the change, the only effectual security against the revival of purchase is to be found in a point of honour like that which prevents its existence in the navy and the civil service ; and a prevailing sense on the part of the officers of the army that they have been justly and liberally dealt with, is an indispensable condition of the growth of such an honourable feeling. .It would be well, both for our national reputation and for the interests of all concerned, to take advantage of the present time, when the subject would be gone into with a full determination to satisfy every equitable claim. We know from experience that the purchase system collapses on the first breaking out of a serious war. We do not know what view the coming demo-cracy may take of a plutocracy which bars their way to an open career in their own national army, which is maintained by them at an expense of 15½ millions a year. Some consideration is also due to the large class of officers who, not having the means of pur-chasing, suffer from the system of promotion by pur-chase. Military discipline prevents them from openly making complaints which would be displeasing to their military chiefs, and the representatives of the army in Parliament belong to the fortunate class who have profited by purchase. There is a fallacy underlying the assertion so constantly repeated, that even officers who have not the means of purchasing their commissions are yet in favour of maintaining the system of purchase. Some, no doubt, are influenced by the hope that when they do at last, or by some lucky chance, obtain a step of rank, they will thereby realise capital in their new commissions; but who will pretend to asseit that officers are indifferent to having their juniors promoted over their heads merely because they cannot themselves produce a certain sum of money? A very slight knowledge of human nature, and of the characteristic qualities of British officers, will show the superior correctness of Lord Clyde's view:—

Do you think that the system of promotion by purchase has an injurious effect upon the army, by dispiriting many excellent officers, who find themselves passed over?—As regards those individuals who have been passed over, certainly. I have known many very estimable men, having higher qualities as officers than usual, men of real promise and merit, and well educated, but who could not purchase; when such men were purchased over, their ardour cooled, and they frequently left the service; or, when they continued, it was from necessity, and not from any love of the profession.*

In the pamphlet published by me last year on the purchase system I pointed out (page 61–3) that the hardship to the non-purchase officers had been much increased since the Crimean War by the Secretary of State having himself engaged in the traffic of

* Evidence taken before the Purchase Commission; Question and Answer 3377.

commissions on a great scale, by means of the Military Reserve Fund:—

In order [I said] to assist the promotion of cavalry officers, to save the public from an excessive increase of the half-pay list, and to get rid of purchase in particular corps, the prizes, which the less wealthy and more professional class of officers have been accustomed to look forward to as the reward of long and good service, are curtailed, and the purchase system is strengthened and extended in a more complete manner throughout the army, by a Government agency operating through a fund constantly supplied by heavy payments from military officers or their families.

Since that a Select Committee of the House of Commons, of which Lord Hotham was chairman, has made a report (a copy of which will be found in the Appendix I., page 69) recommending that the Military Reserve Fund 'should be wound up,' and that 'all payments which may hereafter be made, for purposes now charged on the Reserve Fund, be defrayed from monies appropriated to such purposes by Parliament, and that any future receipts, together with the balance at the credit of the fund, be paid into the Exchequer.' The interests of the hard-working, professional class of officers will thus be placed under the immediate guardianship of Parliament, until, by the abolition of purchase, professional advancement shall become dependent only upon professional claims. At present there is a positive official distinction between rich and poor officers; and until this is obliterated Parliament must interfere in cases of more than usual hardship to protect those who, whatever claims they may have on the grounds of service, personal ability, and professional attainments, cannot produce the prescribed money qualification.

In the same pamphlet I observed (page 68–9) that the basis of the purchase system is quite unequal to such a superstructure as the staff corps of the three Indian Presidencies. According to a memorandum recently issued by the Adjutant-General, officers finally transferred to these staff corps are to receive ' the exact sum such officers would have received under War-Office regulations, had they retired from the service by the sale of their commissions at the time of joining the staff corps as probationers.' This palliative is applied, through the Military Reserve Fund, at the expense of the regimental officers; for the memorandum goes on: ' Promotions in succession to vacancies caused by transfers to the Indian Staff Corps will, in future, be by purchase instead of without purchase, as heretofore, when the officers so transferred are entitled to receive the value of their commissions.'

When Lord Grey was examined before the Purchase Commission, he said:—' My own conviction is, if you touch the system of purchase at all, it would be wiser to abolish it altogether;' and his Royal Highness the Commander-in-Chief, still more emphatically:—

I am quite prepared to say this, that any change that is propounded should be a complete one, and not a partial one. . . . I should be sorry to see any partial change adopted. I think that any change should comprise the whole question, so that there might be security to the officers of the army, for any partial change would lead to doubt and uncertainty.

There were solid grounds for these opinions. This is not one of the cases in which 'half is better than the whole.' On the contrary, the circumstances are such that any partial operation must end in failure. If purchase were only abolished above the rank of captain, that rank would become in a peculiar sense the stepping-stone to advancement to the higher grades, and its early attainment would be the great object of officers with money. The consequence would be that larger sums than ever would be paid for the successive steps of lieutenant and captain, and the outlay which is now spread over four ranks would be accumulated on two; or, if the rank of ensign were abolished, on one. At present, field officers recover a portion of the sums they have paid for their commissions by going on half-pay after twenty-five years' service, which captains could not do, and their outlay would therefore be all lost to them. According to a well-known natural law, if traffic in any article is permitted at all, nothing can prevent the full market value from being given. Purchase may be altogether rooted out of the army, as it has been out of the civil service, by an absolute prohibition, known to have been given in earnest, and backed by a prevailing public opinion both in and out of the profession; but if the principle of purchase has the sanction of authority to however limited a degree, the practice will have an irresistible tendency to increase, in spite of prohibitions and declarations upon honour, until the whole service becomes venal. The utter failure of the endeavours to check payments in excess of regulation, and to prevent the extension of purchase to the adjutancies of Militia and Volunteers, are cases in point.

Exaggerated estimates have been made of the compensation which would have to be paid supposing the entire abolition of purchase to be determined upon. These calculations were based upon the return of seven millions sterling in the appendix of the report of the Purchase Commission, without adverting to the fact that the whole seven millions could not be called for unless the army was entirely disbanded. The return showed the whole value of all the commissions; but, according to the regulations and custom of the service, only officers who retire from the army by sale recover the price of their commissions, while those who remain in the army and are promoted to be major-generals, or who retire on full pay, or take civil appointments connected with the army, have no such advantage.

The committee appointed by the Secretary of State for War in 1857, to report upon the proposals made by me to the Purchase Commission, framed their estimate on the last-mentioned principle :—

According to a parliamentary return (No. 2 of the Appendix to the *Report on the Sale and Purchase of Commissions*), the gross value of the commissions of officers then serving amounted to £7,126,030. But it is impossible to estimate exactly the number of officers who would be disposed to avail themselves of the opportunity of selling their commissions to the public in preference to continuing to serve under the proposed arrangement. We have, however, calculated the probable amount in the best manner we are able, and have arrived at a total of £2,355,288, which would allow of about one-third of the whole number retiring.*

This sum only includes the regulation prices, and adding one-third for the extra prices, the compensation amounts to £3,140,384.

There were 664 retirements by sale during the twenty-four months which immediately preceded the Crimean war. This gives an annual rate of 332 retirements, and £753,000 as the price of the commissions, including the extra price. According to Hart's army list, the retirements by sale of commissions were 399 in 1866, and 425 in 1867. Retirements entitling to compensation would be largest in the first year, because those who retired at once would receive the full value of what they gave up; whereas, as time went on, promotions would take place without purchase to fill the vacancies occasioned by these retirements and by other causes; and the officers who retired by sale at a later period, after having been so promoted, would only receive the value of the commissions to which they had attained up to the date when the purchase system was abolished. There would, therefore, be an increased tendency every year to look forward to promotion or full-pay retirement, instead of looking back to retiring with the value of the commissions which had been acquired under the purchase system, until the claims to retire on that footing entirely ceased. Every additional advantage

* Parliamentary Paper 'Army (Purchase of Commissions),' 498, of 1858; page 8.

given to military officers would diminish the amount to be paid in compensation, by inducing a greater number to remain. Promotion without purchase, increased rates of pay and improved conditions of full pay retirement, would strengthen the motives for continuing in the service ; and, although some officers would retire, others would stay to succeed to the vacancies. There would, therefore, be a self-adjusting process which would have much influence in diminishing the retirements. Regarded as a basis for estimating the amount of the compensation, the annual retirements by sale are liable to a considerable deduction on account of commissions obtained without purchase, upon which only the regulated rate of £100 for every year of foreign, and £50 for every year of home service, would be allowed.

Whatever the amount of the compensation may be, it ought not to be exclusively charged to the existing tax-payers. The compensation is the arrear caused by the neglect of past generations, who have thrown upon military officers the burden of providing their own retirements, and all future generations will participate in the benefits of the organic change by which this defect in the constitution of the army will be remedied. Equity therefore requires that, while the current expense of the revised system should be defrayed by annual grants of Parliament, the cost of making the change should, like the expense of the fortifications and of the reconstruction of the public offices, be spread over a considerable period.

It will be asked how far the ordinary current charge

for the army is likely to be increased or diminished by the proposed changes?

The charge for full pay retirements will, of course, be increased, although not to the extent which has been sometimes feared. The habit which distinguishes our English youth of the upper class, of passing a few years in the army before they marry or succeed to their estates, was not caused by purchase, and is not likely to be diminished by the abolition of it. Many officers would, therefore, retire before they became entitled to a pension, while others would remain after they became entitled, in order to obtain the higher professional rewards. Pensions are, after all, applicable only to a certain limited class of officers who, after having passed twenty-five years in the service, determine not to continue in it to the end.

The rates of pay will be increased, but the annual charge for pay and half-pay, taken together, will be diminished. The proportion of officers to men in our army greatly exceeds that in any other European army and in our own corps of Royal Artillery,* and the time to reduce this proportion will be when, on the one hand, the average efficiency of our officers shall be raised by increasing their pay, relieving them from the burden of purchase, and requiring from them a previous professional training, either at a military college or in

* British army, 1 officer to 28 men.
French ,, 1 ,, 33 ,,
Austrian ,, 1 ,, 40 ,,
Prussian ,, 1 ,, 49 ,,
British Artillery, 1 ,, 35 ,,

C

the ranks, and, on the other hand, the educated and respectable classes shall be attracted into the ranks by making the opening of the higher promotion coincident with the abolition of our indefensible system of recruiting, and with such a degree of attention to the character of recruits as will prevent the admission of reprobates and deserters.

. If the degree to which the public money is wasted, and the standard of efficiency is lowered by. the absence of any proper arrangements to secure fully educated candidates for commissions, and to give them the necessary professional training, was generally understood, there would be an imperative demand for reform. This is a point on which I shall confine myself to quoting statements which have been made by military officers of high character, who will be accepted as authorities on the subject.

Captain R. W. Phipps, Royal Artillery.

The candidate then enters the service as an ensign; at first he is treated as a recruit, and does no duty. When he does escape from the yoke of the drill-sergeant he has very unimportant duties to perform, and does no work except under a senior officer. On an .average, he passes about three years in this capacity. . . . As lieutenant, with little more responsibility, he serves for about six years.*

Major-General Lord West, C.B.

2514. In point of fact, speaking of the line generally and not of the scientific branches of the service, is the professional knowledge which junior officers have an opportunity of acquiring in time of peace, considerable or small?—I think that junior officers have no opportunity at all in the British army; indeed, it is very

---

* *Our Sham Army, and how to make it a Real One.* Longmans, 1868. The extracts which follow are from the evidence delivered before the Purchase Commission.

difficult to make them acquire even the commonest regimental drill, till they have been three or four years in the service.

2515. You have had some practical experience of that in the Crimea?—Yes. When I was commanding a regiment before Sebastopol, from sickness and casualties the number of duty officers became very small, and I then urgently requested that some of a number of young officers, who were kicking their heels at the depôt, might be sent out to head-quarters forthwith. I received 10 of those young officers in a batch, who did not know their right hand from their left, and had never been drilled; I was obliged to send them to the trenches, to different points, in command of parties of 30 or 40 men, much as I objected to leave such parties under the command of such very young subalterns. All that I could do with those officers was this: I sent the adjutant on parade, and told him to show them how to march their men off the ground. All that I could say to them was, 'If the enemy comes on, hold your ground, and drive them back if you can.' In such a case, much was left to the steadiness of the non-commissioned officers and the old soldiers.

2516. In point of fact, those young officers had no more knowledge of professional duties than if they had been so many civilians?—Not a bit more.

2520. The purchase system has prevented a system of previous military training before young men are advanced to the grade and position of officers, and for this reason, that if the education of those young men was protracted to a later period, with the price of the first commission superadded, the expense would be very heavy.

2522. (*Mr. G. Carr Glyn.*) You do not say that that is a consequence of the purchase system, but that it is an abuse of it?—I think it is a consequence of the purchase system. The object is to take boys as early as possible from school, and get them into the army.

Colonel (afterwards Major-General Sir Thomas) Franks.

3269. Have you given your attention to the system of purchase in the army?—Yes.

3270. Have you formed any opinions upon that subject?—My opinions are very strongly against purchase.

3271. Will you state your reasons?—Because I am perfectly satisfied that as long as money is made the chief means of advancement in the army in place of merit, parents will not give their sons so good an education as for other professions.

3284. What other objections have you to purchase, than that it either interferes with the education of young officers or their prospect of advancement in their profession?—I think if parents, as I said before, had the encouragement of merit being rewarded, and also having the money which they lay out in the purchase of commissions, it might be an inducement to spend that money, and it would be spent in better educating young men previously to entering into the service.

3300. In what way would you do away with influence?—By rewarding merit and merit alone.

3303. (*Sir Harry D. Jones.*) What would be your scheme for promotion in peace; by merit you mean, I presume, an officer who has distinguished himself in the field?—No. In time of peace an officer should be promoted who had prepared himself for a time of war by education, and acquirements, and attention to the service.

3304. (*Mr. E. Ellice.*) Do you think that a British regiment of infantry is a much worse instrument than a regiment of infantry in any other service?—I believe that in the field our infantry is perhaps the finest infantry in the world when it has gone through the ordeal of service; but I think, on going into the field at first, both our infantry and our cavalry, in consequence of the ignorance of our officers, appear to a very great disadvantage. I am speaking generally of our young officers.

3318. Do you consider that officers who have purchased are not so efficient as those officers who have not purchased?—Yes; I think if a man knows that with very little attention and a little smattering of knowledge, and lots of money, he is certain to get on, he is not likely to pay proper attention to his duties.

3319. (*Mr. E. Ellice.*) Did you find the officers who purchased in your regiment inefficient?—An officer who knows that very little attention and a large fortune will enable him to rise regimentally to the head of his regiment, is not likely to trouble himself much about increasing his own professional knowledge.

Lord Clyde.

3392. With respect to entrance into the army, purchase being abolished, upon what principle do you think officers should be first appointed to commissions?—There should be a higher standard of education than is exacted at present. I presume that the parents or relatives who would take care to fit a youth to pass the standard which I conceive would be necessary, would have imposed upon them the necessity of keeping him at school at least to the age of seventeen or eighteen, with very rare exceptions of remarkably quick boys; but that implies, in my idea, the possession of property, which I deem also of moment; the very fact of the relations of a boy being able to maintain a candidate at a college up to the age of eighteen, would ally him with property; and I think if you established a high standard of examination you would then improve the officers in the army.

3393. Admitting the standard of education, how would you select from persons equally educated for appointments?—In the same way as I presume they do at Woolwich; those who pass the best examination should be chosen for commissions.

3394. Then you would confine the first entrances into the army to a competitive examination?—Certainly.

3395. Having obtained the first entrance into the army, how would you have the promotion go on in the subordinate ranks before you came to field rank?—I think there is one thing very much wanted, that instead of at once appointing a young man who shall have passed such an examination as we are now adverting to, he should be a cadet first, and he should learn all the duties of a soldier and a non-commissioned officer, and that he should not get his commission until he has proved himself fit for it. When those young men first join a corps, the commanding officer is very likely in India, and they are at the depôt at home, and those young men should go through that second education before they had commissions, and the selection should be from those young men who showed the greatest zeal, and had improved themselves most in the knowledge of their duties so as to fit them for officers.

3396. Who had in fact the greatest amount of professional attainments?—Yes; and who had attained that during this period.

More important in a merely financial point of view will be the savings consequent upon a return to the sound principle of promoting only to vacancies on a fixed establishment, and upon the restoration of the half-pay list to its original object of making a provision for reduced and invalided officers. The supplementary line of promotion known as the 'unattached list,' which has arisen from the necessity of compensating both those who have paid heavily for their commissions and those who have been passed over for want of the means of payment, has swelled the annual charge for half-pay to £331,500; and, in its bearing upon the interests of the officers, it has produced a state of plethora and stagnation which could not be exceeded in any non-purchase corps. There are 354 colonels, exclusive of India and of the Artillery and Engineers; and, after allowing for deaths among the colonels, and for retirements by sale of those who do not choose to wait, the colonel last added to the list cannot, at the rate at which vacancies occur on the establishment of major-generals, be promoted in less than twenty-five years. Indeed this is an understatement, for a considerable proportion of the names on the fixed establishment of general officers still belong to the period of the great war, and when these are succeeded by the much younger men lower down the list, the annual casualties will be less than at present. There is also a great redundancy in the ranks of lieutenant-colonel and major. This excessive development, intended originally to quicken promotion, has ended in being a great obstruction to it, from the impossibility of the increased numbers being absorbed in the higher ranks within a reasonable time.

The inevitable tendency of these abnormal arrangements is to cause an accumulation of field officers quite disproportioned to the numbers of the lower ranks, and all the grades—colonels, lieutenant-colonels, and majors—are choked and brought to a state of stagnation. Then there is the prevailing impression, which used to be quoted by high authorities as an incontrovertible maxim, that as our officers pay for their commissions more than they receive from them, and provide for their own retirement, they are the cheapest body of officers in Europe. From this naturally followed the disposition to be lavish in the use of that which could be easily, and, as it was imagined, cheaply obtained. Officers of the three field ranks are employed on the staff and in a great variety of administrative and other situations at home and abroad, with a profusion unknown to any other system, and yet great numbers remain unemployed. The large sums invested in commissions also stand in the way of the reductions which ought to be made according to the varying circumstances of the service, a constantly recurring instance of which is the difficulty experienced in disposing of the supernumerary officers on the return of a regiment from India. We have at this moment a striking example of the obstacle which purchase opposes to the introduction of improvements into our military system. It has been considered advisable that future appointments to the regimental depôts should be made only on a five years' tenure, and the immediate effect of this ordinary salutary rule upon this division of the commission market has been to reduce the value of the invested capital as follows:—

It [the War Office Circular of the 16th December 1866] pretends to preserve vested interests by permitting the officers now in the depôt battalions to retain their present appointments unaffected by the five years'. tenure, which is, to be applied to their successors, and also to them on promotion.

But as no man can purchase with half-pay in five years before him, and no man will exchange into them for the same reason, it follows that 46 out of the 47 officers now in the depôt battalions have been practically deprived of the right of purchase and exchange they enjoyed in the regiments they came from, together with the hopes of promotion such privileges held out.

They entered the depôt battalion service under these conditions, and having been caught, they are robbed of the inducements that made them leave their regiments.

The actual money value of which the majors alone have been deprived may be set down at £28,800.

The sum required to effect an exchange into the depôt battalion as major was about £600; the sum now required to get *out* would be £1,000; multiply this £1,600 by the 18 majors, and we have the sum of £28,800.

This is only another illustration of the familiar truth, that it is bad economy for an employer to endeavour to give less than the fair value of the services he receives. In the end he always has to pay more, and is worse served, than if he had begun by taking care that his servants were properly paid.

If the Government accepts the obligation of relieving its officers from the heavy mulcts to which they are subjected by the purchase system, and of giving them pay and retiring pensions sufficient for their subsistence, the value of the British officer will at once become apparent, and a desire will be felt to improve such costly agency, and to make it go as far as possible. A new spirit of economy will arise in all that relates to the administration of the army. No difficulty will then be felt in arranging that commissions shall be given only to persons who have proved their qualifications, either in the ranks or in a military college, and only in the numbers required for an army voluntary in a true and high sense—not one got together by intoxication, cajoling, and bounty,* and kept together by flogging and branding. The junior ranks will then be in such just proportion to the higher that promotion will proceed in a continuous stream, and future obstruction will be prevented by returning to the practice of promoting only to vacancies on a fixed establishment, and of confining the half-pay list to the object of providing for reduced and invalided officers.

Another class of savings combines pecuniary economy with increased simplicity and facility of administration. Of this description is the consolidation with the proposed higher rates of pay, of numerous miscellaneous allowances in money or kind, the issue of which in a separate form increases the complication, expense and delay of military administration, without conferring any benefit on the officer;† and the discon-

---

* 'We get our men, with difficulty, by every kind of cajoling and inducement we can devise ; and, in our necessity, descend to those means which men do not have recourse to till they think all others are exhausted.'
—*Sidney Herbert.*

'The present system of recruiting rather seeks to inveigle young men into the army than, by a fair representation of military service, and an honest and open declaration of the advantages which a military career presents, to hold up the army as a profession, of which a fair proportion of those who are capable of bearing arms might well avail themselves.'—
Lord Dalhousie, Lord Eversley, the Adjutant-General Lord W. Paulet, and the other Commissioners for inquiring into the Recruiting of the Army, 1867.

† This remark does not apply to the colonial money allowances given in addition to regimental pay in certain colonies where provisions, forage, house-rent, &c., are much more expensive than in the United Kingdom or at other stations.

tinuance of all official connection with the army agents (the authorised brokers and stakeholders of the purchase system), who are paid £41,000 a year for doing in duplicate what must under any circumstances be done in a more simple and direct manner by the public establishments. At this heavy annual charge we purchase double accounts, complication, delay, and insecurity. On the other hand, if 'a band of music is essential to the credit and appearance of a regiment,' as stated in the Queen's Regulations, the public and not the officers should pay for it; and when forage or other allowances in kind are necessary, they should not be made the subject of constantly-recurring money transactions, but they should be given free, and their average value should be deducted in fixing the new rates of pay. A more important reform would be the substitution of a net rate of soldier's pay for the 'stoppage system,' the last excuse for which has ceased with the creation of a body of supervising officers, one of whose duties it will be to verify the numbers requiring the issue of rations. The consolidation of 'beer money' with pay, both in the regular army and the militia, would efface a degrading reminiscence of a bygone state of manners.

Lastly, if the modifications of the existing system advocated by me are adopted, bounty-money, levy-money and bringing-money may be discontinued, and the expense of recruiting may be limited to providing proper places in each district for the reception of recruits, and to the free kit and uniform which must, under any circumstances, be given. The expense of the ' administration of martial law,' the details of which are shown in a note,* will also be greatly diminished when we get rid of the handful of confirmed tipplers and irreclaimable scamps who make a trade of deserting, and are repeatedly committing offences which lead to their trial by courts martial and to their passing a considerable portion of their service in prison. The loss of service during desertion and imprisonment, as well as the further loss caused by escorts, guards, and frequent courts of enquiry and courts-martial, will be saved; the men will be ' effective ' in a much greater proportion than at present; and the expenditure on hospitals and medical attendance will be reduced in more ways than can be properly described. Intemperance and vice—not climate and hard service—are the principal causes of sickness,

*	1868–69	1867–68
	£	£
Pay, &c., of Establishment of Judge Advocate General	5,125	5,000
Contingencies of Establishment of Judge Advocate General	1,050	1,000
Allowances to Acting Judge Advocates, and other expenses of Courts Martial	2,000	2,000
Pay, &c., of Establishments of Military Prisons	23,113	23,194
Contingencies of Military Prisons . .	1,156	1,260
Subsistence, clothing, stores, and expenses for men confined in Military Prisons .	24,139	23,646
Expenses of confinement of men in Civil Gaols	4,000	4,000
Expenses of confinement of men in Barrack Cells	14,860	15,000
Expenses incurred in the apprehension and conviction of Deserters, &c. .	13,270	12,270
	88,713	87,370

mortality, and invaliding in the army, and the greatest saving of all will be the substitution of the elevating influences connected with a short term of service and a reasonable prospect of promotion, for the depressing and corrupting influences associated with our disgraceful system of recruiting and the protracted bachelorhood of our long terms of service.

On the whole, I am confident that, provided the readjustments properly consequent upon the abolition of purchase are made, the actual army grant of £15,455,400 will more than suffice for defraying the current charges of the revised system.

IV.

TERM OF THE SOLDIER'S SERVICE, AND CONSTITUTION OF THE ARMY OF RESERVE.

I have now come to the end of that part of our military system which has been heretofore treated by me, and I would gladly stop at this point. But 'necessity' *has* 'enforced a change,' and we *must* 'fit the rest to it'; for this is evidently one of the cases in which 'it is safer to change many things than one.' If the abolition of purchase is the preliminary condition of any real reform of our army, the reduction of the term of service of our soldiers, and the remoulding of the militia so as to make it a suitable body for the reception and assimilation of the time-expired men, are its indispensable complement.

A very small proportion of the Duke of Wellington's

army, 'which could go anywhere and do anything,' was composed of men of more than five years' service; and a man who had served two campaigns was considered an old soldier. In Napoleon's early successful days, his *corps d'élite* were composed of soldiers old by experience of war rather than by age ; but, as he approached his downfall, he was forced to look to quantity rather than to quality, and great efforts were made to retain old soldiers, who had become too old, and to multiply young soldiers, who were sent to join the army before they had been properly trained. According to General Trochu,* French soldiers reach their maximum efficiency for active service after from two to four years' experience; and although the non-commissioned officers may with advantage be somewhat older, regiments should undergo a gradual process of renovation, so that their spirit and traditions may be preserved by a small number of old soldiers. Service in the French army has been reduced from seven to five years, with a further period of four years in the reserve. The term of service in Austria is six years in the line, three in the first reserve, and the same in the second. The line and the first reserve form the field force. The second reserve is intended for garrison duty, but, if necessary, can be sent into the field. Men of education may serve as one year's volunteers, and if able to pass an examination, they

* See the chapters, ' Jeunes soldats et vieux soldats,' and ' Les grognards du premier empire,' in Trochu's charming treatise, *L'Armée Française en* 1867. This is Kinglake's ' Colonel Trochu, the officer understood to be entrusted by the Emperor with the function of advising at the French headquarters.'

may be appointed officers of reserve. Every Prussian serves three years in the regiment,* four in the reserve of the regiment (the man remaining on the rolls liable to be called on for active service, if required), and five in the first class of the landwehr; the two latter bodies being only called out for occasional drill in time of peace. Volunteers who wish to follow other professions may serve a year in the ranks, after which they pass into the landwehr.

According to the evidence delivered before the Recruiting Commissioners of 1861 and 1867, a soldier begins to fall off after twelve years' service, and is generally worn out after sixteen or seventeen. The highest estimate gives eighteen years as the limit of efficiency for active service. The Duke of Cambridge says, ' The best soldier is a man after three years' service, and from that to about twelve or fourteen years' service, and I think even to sixteen.' Colonel Fitz-Wygram, commanding the 15th Hussars, would ' like to see every man go at the end of twelve years.' In his regiment he had not a single man of fourteen years' service who was at his duty. ' Cavalry regiments get no good work out of their men after fourteen years' service:' ' men get nervous about riding,' and ' after that time they will get into any berth, in order to get out of riding.' The position in which

---

* The following testimony was borne by Colonel Walker, C.B., Military Attaché at Berlin, in a recent lecture on the battle of Königsgrätz : ' I was much struck with the cheeriness with which these young soldiers went into action for the second time. All *recruits* fight well in their first battle; those who afterwards brave death and wounds with cheerfulness are *soldiers*.'

our army has been placed by the re-enlistment, in the face of this evidence, of 30,000 ten years' infantry, and twelve years' cavalry men, requires no comment. The rapid disintegration of the regular army in the first active campaign, and the consequent necessity for increasing in still larger proportion the large re-cruiting which always accompanies the breaking out of war, must seriously aggravate the difficulties of the crisis.

But bare, abstract military efficiency is by no means the only, nor, all things considered, the most important point of view. During the first few years of his service the recruit gains more than he loses, even with reference to the qualifications for civil life. His *physique* rapidly improves under the influence of good food, clothing, and lodging. Drill and gymnas-tics give him suppleness of limb and an erect, manly demeanour. He acquires a sense of duty and a just appreciation of the value of character, and he learns both to obey and to command. Foreign service and a variety of society give him knowledge of the world, such as the youth of the upper classes obtain by means of the universities and foreign travel. If he returns to civil life within a reasonable time, before the stiffness grows upon him which characterises those who have long borne arms, he has no difficulty in resuming industrial habits, and he is certain to be in re-quest for a great variety of occupations implying trust and method. The inordinate length of the first term of service is the only real obstacle to the employment of time-expired men in large classes of subordinate appointments in the Customs, Inland Revenue, and various other public departments, besides the metropolitan, municipal, and county police, the Irish constabulary, and the great railway establishments, for all which there could not be a better training than a *few* years' service in the army.* It is superfluous to point out how full of advantage to the recruiting of the army, to the good conduct and educational improvement of the men, and to the efficiency of our public and quasi-public establishments, the systematic employment of time-expired seven years' men would be. An army which receives annually a portion of the population, and restores an equivalent number trained as I have described, is a powerful instrument of national education in a large and high sense. It would be to the body of the people much more than our universities are to the upper class.

I will not complete the picture by describing the sort of character usually formed by prolonged barrack life, the bad example of old soldiers, and the absence of those natural influences which maintain the healthy tone and self-respect of the ordinary social state. There is a remarkable paragraph in the report of Colonel Henderson, R.E., the Inspector-General of Military Prisons, for 1865 :—

* Great as have been the benefits which our nation has derived from the military qualities of the Irish people, we have yet to see the effect upon the efficiency of the army and the consolidation of the empire of really offering a military career to a race which has freely shed its blood in the service of Spain, France, and, more lately, of the United States of America, and of accustoming them to regard enlistment in the army as a means of ultimately attaining to an honourable and comfortable position in their beloved native country.

The statistics of the prisons show a considerable increase over the two previous years in the number of prisoners in confinement: during the year 1865, there were 6,390 as against 5,470 in the previous year. The principal increase is among soldiers whose services were from seven to fourteen years, of whom 2,166 were sentenced in 1865 against 1,325 in the preceding year; indeed, it may be remarked that the increase of commitments, among this class of soldiers, has been steadily progressive from 335 in 1859 to 2,166 in 1865. It might, perhaps, be desirable that some investigation into this great increase in a particular class should be made.

The phenomenon is explained by the causes to which allusion has been made. When a soldier has nothing more to learn, and is no longer influenced by the prospect of returning to civil life, he generally loses heart, and begins to deteriorate. Those men only should be allowed to bind themselves to military service as their profession for life who are actuated by real professional motives, and are well qualified to perform their part in the non-commissioned or commissioned ranks.

A correct general impression of this state of things prevails throughout the country, and hence the strong objections held by respectable working men to enlist except under the influence of some disappointment, and the extreme dislike with which respectable parents regard the enlistment of their sons. Twelve years appear a lifetime to a young man of eighteen. To enter into an engagement for twelve years is, in his view, selling himself into bondage—and truly so it is, for the period is sufficiently long effectually to detach him from the habits and associations of ordinary life, and to recast him in a peculiar mould from which

he can never escape. If we desire to make the army
popular, and to attract a better class of recruits, we
must reduce the term of service.

But the greatest benefit of short service has yet to
be mentioned. No degree of administrative skill can
make a general permission to marry compatible with
military efficiency,* and the long periods of service
hitherto in vogue have therefore made our army a
school of immorality, the evil effects of which have
overflowed upon our civil population. A happy
change would take place if the first term of service
were reduced from twelve to seven years. Entering
the army at eighteen or nineteen, our young men would,
in that case, generally leave it at twenty-five or
twenty-six, which is the best age for marrying; and
the few picked men who would be retained should all
be allowed to marry, as one of the advantages of their
position. Soldiers seldom marry in the earlier stages
of their career. Between twenty and twenty-five
years of age, only about 10·4 per cent. are married,
so that the present regulated proportion, including
that authorised for the non-commissioned officers,
would suffice for the reduced term of service. After
that the proportion of married men to age in our
army is as follows: twenty-five to thirty, 24·8 per
cent.; thirty to thirty-five, 37 per cent.; and above
forty, 48·3 per cent. This state of things is, as an
ordinary condition of service, totally incompatible

* This will be abundantly evident from the articles from the Queen's
Regulations and Orders for the Army in the Appendix (II., page 74).
It would be difficult to match the portentous naïveté of the marginal
description of the first article. 'Marriages to be discouraged.'

with military efficiency, but it is not unsuited to the plan of permitting a few first-rate soldiers, chiefly non-commissioned officers, to re-engage with a higher rate of pay, a pension on retirement, and unlimited permission to marry.

The following return, which has been kindly furnished to me by the Registrar-General, has a grave significance in-connection with this part of the subject:—

ENGLAND AND WALES.

Proportion of husbands to 100 males living in 1861 of all conditions.

AGES.			AGES.		
15—20 .	.	·5	40—45 .	.	82·6
20—25 .	.	22·3	45—50 .	.	83·1
25—30 .	.	58·7	50—55 .	.	81·0
30—35 .	.	75·5	55—60 .	.	78·9
35—40 .	.	81·7			

See Census Report of 1861, vol. iii. p. 118.

GEORGE GRAHAM,
Registrar-General.

General Register Office,
Somerset House,
16 June 1868.

These, therefore, are the proportions in which soldiers of the different ages would marry if they were allowed to follow their natural instincts and affections.

The deteriorating effect of prolonged military service is also shown by the fact that while, under 25 years of age, the mortality in the army is lower than it is among the male civil population, above that age a change for the worse takes place, and the mortality increases with the advance of years in a much more rapid ratio than in civil life, although soldiers' lives were originally all picked lives, the recruits having been subjected to a careful medical examination before they were passed into the service. A comparison of the latter steps in the following scale has a painful significance to those who are accustomed to the examination of such statistics:—

Annual ratio of Deaths per 1,000 living: (1) among troops serving in the United Kingdom, 1859–65; (2) among the civil male population of England and Wales by English life table; and (3) among the male population of the 63 Healthiest Districts of England and Wales 1849–53 :—

AGES.	AVERAGE ANNUAL RATE OF MORTALITY.		
	Of Troops serving in the United Kingdom 1859–65.	Of the Civil Male Population of England and Wales by English Life Table.*	Of Males in 63 of the Healthiest Districts of England and Wales. 1849–53.†
Under 20	3·07	6·89	5·83
20 — 25	5·80	8·68	7·30
25 — 30	7·99	9·55	7·93
30 — 35	12·03	10·56	8·36
35 — 40	15·89	11·94	9·00
40 and ups·	18·94	13·96	9·86

* For the 17 years 1838–54.

† There is good reason to believe that the death-rate of the most Healthy Districts, in 1849–53, represents the present mortality of the population living in the healthy parts of England.

GEORGE GRAHAM,
General Register Office,   Registrar-General.
  Somerset House,
    4th July, 1868.

Our pot-house system of recruiting, the soldier's long term of service, and the restrictions upon his marriage, act as a direct encouragement to drunkenness and debauchery in a great national establishment which might, under different arrangements, be con-

verted into a popular training school of the highest
intellectual and moral value.

The charge for soldiers' pensions for 1868-9 is
£1,218,200. Pensions are not offered for the first
term of twelve years' service, and they are therefore
not likely to enter into the calculations of the recruit.
They are practically given, like the second bounty
and free kit, and the extra penny a day, for the sole
purpose of tempting the twelve years' men to re-inlist.
These old soldiers are induced to re-engage, and hold
on for pensions, at an annual cost per man which,
including the value of the pension, is about double
that of young soldiers, and ten times that of reserve
soldiers. According to the annuity tables in the
Postal Guide, the liability which the country incurred
on account of the future pensions of the 30,000 re-
engaged men is equal to a payment of £600,000 a year
from the date of their re-engagement, in excess of
the charge which appears in the estimates while they
are serving. If we adopted the opposite course of
largely reducing the period of compulsory service, and
of requiring all to leave the army at the end of their
first term except men of superior character and sol-
dierlike qualifications—offering to all time-expired
men the alternative of being enrolled in the reserve,
with a liberal retaining fee—the whole of this great
expenditure in pensions, and bounty, and extra pay
(a free kit would be required for the recruit who
would replace the old soldier) would be saved, except
the pensions which would ultimately be given to the
few men of highest character and greatest efficiency,

who would be retained as a favour. With such a saving as this we could afford to make the reserve army for home defence all that it ought to be. 30,000 young soldiers for general service and 30,000 time-expired men for home defence—or 60,000 in all —might be maintained for less than the annual sum which we pay for our 30,000 re-engaged men.

It may perhaps be thought that the requirements of India and the Colonies are inconsistent with this line of action. It is, however, a mistake to suppose that the foreign service which so largely enters into the system of the British army is unfavourable to recruiting. It may deter some, but to the majority of young men it is a decided attraction. The love of travel and adventure is by no means confined to the upper class, and our military service would not be what it is to our people if Canada and Abyssinia, Australia, India, China, and Japan were struck out of the account. The increased knowledge of foreign countries consequent upon the spread of national education has at once stimulated curiosity and calmed apprehension. Colonial service, with the exception of Canada, has been reduced within narrow limits, and it may be still further contracted. Indian service is decidedly popular. Nowhere is the British soldier so liberally treated. His pay is higher, his rations are more varied and abundant, and his facilities for marrying are greater, on the Indian, than on any other station ; and there is a large class of appoint- ments in the Ordnance, Public Works, and other departments in India for which soldiers of good character and fair education are eligible. The case of India is exceptional, and its exigency may be met by exceptional action on the part of the Government of India. There are grave political objections to returning to the plan of having a separate army for India, but these do not apply to that of holding out local inducements to the soldiers serving in India to renew their engagements. Even now, on the return of regiments from India, half the men volunteer for further service with regiments which remain, and this proportion might be increased without any increase of charge, because, for every man who is induced to stay, the expense of two passages is saved —of the man who would otherwise return home, and of the man who would otherwise have to be sent out to relieve him. We need not scruple to encourage Indian re-engagements, for not only is the soldier himself benefited, but these soldiers and their descendants, in the capacity of settlers, largely contribute to the industrial and religious progress of India; and all their weight is thrown into the scale with the English connection.

The engagement with the time-expired men at home should, I think, be for ten years, which would give seventeen years military service in all—seven in the regular army, and ten in the reserve. At the end of that period they should retire, as a matter of course, unless they are invited, on account of special qualifications, to serve for a further term, in which case they would become entitled to a pension on retirement. Prudent men, who hoped to obtain regular civil employment, might, however, object to place themselves under an absolute engagement for ten years to be absent from their homes and work for a certain number of days in each year. Unwilling service is not of any real value. Our object should be to make every branch of the army popular, and to reduce the number of desertions. For these reasons it may be advisable that the men should be able to release themselves from their engagement to the reserve by giving six months' notice. They should be at liberty to join any regiment of the reserve, and if they changed their residence, they should be transferred to another in their new neighbourhood.

If these changes were made, time-expired men from the regular army would annually become available in considerable numbers, and the next question is, how they could be most advantageously disposed of. The obvious course would be to incorporate them with the militia, whereby both classes of soldiers would be combined under one organisation and command, and the militia would be strengthened by a leavening of thoroughly trained soldiers. A large proportion of the time-expired men might be expected to join the militia, but experience shows that few will voluntarily undertake the obligation to return to the ranks, with the liability to distant and prolonged foreign service, to the complete disruption of domestic ties and local occupations. The inducement to retire from the army, when the excitement of youth and the passion for novelty and adventure have been satisfied, is the desire to enter on a settled

life, with all its natural enjoyments, its family affections, and the scope which it furnishes for the ordinary pursuits of peaceful industry.

There are also reasons for believing that a change
must be made in the constitution of the militia which
would render it, to a far greater extent than at
present, a suitable body for the reception of the
time-expired men. If a man be once well trained,
a very short annual exercise suffices to keep him
serviceable, but the militiaman never arrives at this
status. The time allowed in any one year is barely
sufficient to carry him, even in the most superficial
manner, through the many necessary branches of
instruction. All that can be done in the time is
to teach the militia regiments to move in a body.
Proper musketry instruction, which can only be
given individually, is out of the question. The introduction of arms of precision, by giving the character of a skilled profession even to the position of the
private soldier, and making it necessary for him to
acquire, by an elaborate process of teaching, the art
of protecting himself and destroying his enemy, has
rendered the existing conditions of militia service as
obsolete as the rude weapon with which they were
originally associated. The want of proper training
in the officers is still more apparent. Indeed this
valuable old constitutional force has fallen so low
that officers are not to be had in the requisite
number. In the militia, officers are as deficient as
they are redundant in the line. Nearly two-fifths
(1,363 out of 3,485) of all the commissions in the

militia are vacant, and, while some regiments are without any subaltern at all, many have only two or three. Let us not deceive ourselves. It would be the height of rashness and cruelty to place the militia, as it now exists, in the line of battle against troops armed and exercised as regular troops now are. Our national security rests on a totally unreliable foundation, so far as it depends on the militia.

But if, instead of six weeks in the first, and a month in every subsequent year, every militiaman was trained for an entire year *at the beginning of his service*, a few days in each year would keep him in practice. His first engagement should be for one year, after which he should be invited either to enlist in the regular army for seven years, or to join the militia for a term of ten years, terminable at six months' notice. A sufficient number of these recruits should be kept constantly embodied at the head-quarters of the regiment, to supply the vacancies in its ranks, with a liberal margin for those who would be likely to enlist in the line after their year's training was over. Besides the adjutant and musketry instructor, and the non-commissioned officers for teaching drill, a captain instructor should be selected from the regular army for each regiment of militia, whose duty it would be to instruct both the officers and men of the embodied portion of the regiment in the science and practice of their profession. Candidates approved by the Lord-Lieutenant for commissions in the militia should serve at the head-quarters of the regiment until they were certified to be qualified for the duties of a subaltern officer, and promotion to be captain and field officer should be made upon suitable tests of qualification. The existing volunteer officers of each district should be encouraged to go through a similar course of instruction at the head-quarters of the militia regiment, and in future the honour of a commission in the volunteers should only be conferred upon those who have prepared themselves for the efficient performance of the duties.* The depôt battalions should be broken up, and the depôts of the respective regiments of the line should be placed in the same town as the head-quarters of the militia regiments with which they are most intimately connected, and every practicable step should be taken (such as giving them the same number, colours, and uniforms) to strengthen the relations between particular line and militia regiments. They would daily associate in military and athletic exercises, and would go through the same course of instruction and attend the same lectures under the captain-instructor. In short, the county militia regiments should, as far as possible, take the position of second battalions to the county line regiments, and the county yeomanry cavalry and volunteer force should be connected both with line and militia by a liberal relation of comradeship and mutual help. When these or other similar arrangements have been made, the time-expired men from the regular army

* These suggestions do not, of course, apply to officers who receive commissions in the militia or volunteers after having served in the regular army.

may be incorporated with the militia under the same conditions of service as the men enlisted directly into the militia.*

This would be a homogeneous system, all the parts of which would work towards a common end. Instead of the line and militia competing for recruits, as at present, they would give each other mutual support. The militia would pass on young soldiers to the line without impairing its own efficiency, and the line would return mature soldiers, still in the vigour of life, to reinforce the militia. A real and useful connection would be established between the different branches of the military force of the country, and young men volunteering into the line from the militia or volunteers would feel that they were going to serve among neighbours and friends. Contrary to the practice of the other European nations, our reserves are fresh, untrained men, while our regular army is chiefly composed of old professional soldiers. What I propose is to reverse this—to encourage the young unmarried men to enlist in the regular army, and to fill the reserves with trained men who have arrived at an age to settle down in civil life. Line, militia, yeomanry, and volunteers would be organised in a simple and convenient manner under the general commanding the division; and the whole body would be so penetrated with the spirit and experience of the regular army, that the divisional military and administrative staff (which might be strengthened to any necessary extent) could freely operate in support of it.

* For further explanations of these proposals, see Appendix III., p. 75.

The rapidity with which militia regiments have improved after they have been embodied shows that the year's previous training, followed by a week or ten days' annual exercise, would give us the fruit of all our expenditure of time and money—an efficient, reliable militia—which cannot be obtained by any number of repetitions of the existing annual exercises. Our able-bodied youth would be economised and turned to the best account, because the year from eighteen to nineteen is the one which can best be spared in the life of a young man, standing, as he then does, on the edge of the labour market, without having taken up his place in it; and this year spent under discipline and instruction at the militia head-quarters would be well spent, even in reference to success in civil life. Those who have not completed their elementary education should be required to attend the regimental school until they come up to a prescribed standard; and the library and reading-room, and the lectures given by the military instructor and volunteer lecturers, should be open to all. Every militia head-quarters would become a military school, like those which have been established by the Government of Canada at several towns, under officers of the regular army, at which candidates for commissions in their militia are trained until they pass a certain examination, more or less strict according to their rank. Our provincial military schools, however, would be more efficient than those of Canada, because, being based upon a small but permanently embodied military force, they would combine practical with theoretical instruction; and once every year the entire regiment might be called out for brigade and division manœuvres with the other troops of the district. Instead of the holiday displays, which are not self-supporting even for a single day, got up by collecting volunteer regiments from distant parts of the country, the volunteers included in each military division would assemble for their annual exercise with the local line, militia, and yeomanry regiments, and they would all be supported by the local, military, and administrative staff, so that the troops which might have to serve together in war would acquire the habit of acting together under circumstances most resembling those of war; and as not merely the combatant ranks, but *the entire military machine*, would be periodically seen in actual operation, defects would be remedied without loss or discredit, which, in the face of an enemy, might involve untold sacrifices.

The efficiency of an army can only come up to the level of that of its officers, and it is useless to multiply militiamen and volunteers if the officers are unfit for their position. Attention has hitherto been almost exclusively directed to training the men, who can be obtained in any number, and can soon be rendered fit to take their places in the ranks, and we seem to have forgotten for the moment that an army must be officered as well as manned, and that officers require a careful training, and cannot be extemporised in time of need. The right to command troops of all arms conferred by the Queen's Regulations on militia, yeomanry, and volunteer officers will, if these officers are not properly instructed, cause disgraceful and dangerous confusion in the event of its being necessary to take active measures of national defence. The property qualification for commissions in the militia, which is open to many of the objections to purchase, and the practice of billeting the militia upon the public-houses, which is very objectionable on moral as well as on military grounds, should be brought to a final close, and proper militia barracks should be provided in every county; and as military systems have a social as well as a professional aspect, all the other arrangements will be facilitated by the intercourse between the officers of the four forces—line, militia, yeomanry, and volunteers—at the county military club.

Entirely independent reasons exist for breaking up the depôt battalions, and returning to the plan of regimental depôts. The depôt battalions are the worst possible schools for the young officer and the recruit; and there is hardly an officer of rank or standing, except those on the staff of the depôt battalions, who does not dislike and condemn them. Commanding officers of regiments complain that the drafts sent to them are ill-trained, badly drilled, and awkward, while the officers of depôt battalions complain of the non-commissioned officers sent to the depôts. The interests of the officers are conflicting; and it is unwise to commit the first training of the young officers and soldiers to men who, having no connection with their regiments, cannot be expected to take any real interest in them, and are not likely ever to see them again after they have once left the depôt battalions to join their respective regiments.

The 'militia reserve,' authorised last year to be raised to the extent of one-fourth of the quotas fixed by law, hangs fire; but even if the full numbers were obtained, it is doubtful whether the plan would stand the test of experience. It is a new principle to give men all their advantages in time of peace, and to take the chance of their being willing to encounter the hardships and hazards of war at some future indefinite period, long after they have spent their bounty, and have probably married, or entered into other engagements inconsistent with foreign service. Militiamen have always shown the utmost readiness to join the line for active service; and if the term of service is reduced, and the gulf which separates the non-commissioned from the commissioned ranks is bridged over, the regular army will become so popular, and such satisfactory relations will be established between it and the militia and volunteers, that, although the latter will be enrolled only for home service, there will be no want of men offering for the line from among those who happen, when their country requires their services, to be free to enter into new engagements. Payments in advance for future contingent foreign service will fail to secure men when we most want them. Our real reserve is the spontaneous readiness which Englishmen have always shown to join the ranks when there is a prospect of active service; and building upon this foundation, we ought to remove the objections justly felt by parents to the enlistment of their sons, and to make the army more than ever an object of desire to our youth. If any special inducement is necessary, it should be given to those who actually come forward to meet the emergency; but I do not believe that it will be necessary. In proportion as the home army is filled with time-expired seven years' men, it will be safer and easier to induce the recruits to join the general service army.

According to the numerical returns of enlistments submitted to Parliament by the Adjutant-General during the years of war from 1805 to 1814, while 121,622 men were obtained by common recruiting, 113,409 were supplied by volunteers from the militia. The real recruiting question is how the first step to the military profession can best be got over:

The point of difficulty [Baron Dupin observed in his report upon the military force of Great Britain], in recruiting in towns or the country, is to draw a man from the spot of his birth, the roof of his father, the ties of his infancy; to tear him, amongst entreaties, tears and imprecations, from all that he most loves and reverences upon earth. But the young soldier who is already formed by the regular militia service has assumed the uniform and quitted his paternal habitation. He soon quits also the vicinity of his birth-place; he inhabits a barrack where there are no associations but those of military life. Warmly clad, comfortably lodged, and better fed than any other soldier in Europe, his situation is, in every respect, very supportable. There is awakened in the bosom of the militiaman the sentiment of national honour and glory, the hope of promotion and the desire of reward.

It is neither necessary nor desirable that the change from the old to the new constitution of the militia should take place simultaneously in every part of the country. All the counties might not be equally prepared for it, nor could the regular army furnish at once the requisite number of professionally trained officers to act as musketry instructors and captain instructors. The best way of making the change will be by military divisions. The militia should not again be assembled on the old footing in the divisions selected for reorganisation. The general commanding should consult with the lord-lieutenants to what extent each regiment should be partially embodied under the new terms of service, until all the men belonging to it are trained by successive annual reliefs; and every necessary arrangement should be made to form the line, militia, yeomanry, and volunteers of the division into a single organised body, annually assembled for a few days' exercise, and capable of taking the field at very short notice, supported by a full proportion of military and administrative staff.

eechesonarmyre꤮trev

APPENDIX.

APPENDIX I.

[See p. 27.]

REPORT OF THE SELECT COMMITTEE ON MILITARY RESERVE FUNDS.

The Select Committee appointed to enquire into ' The origin of the Military Reserve Funds, the sources from which they are derived, and the objects to which they are applied,' have considered the matters to them referred, and have agreed to the following Report.

1. The Military Reserve Funds comprise what is generally called the Army Reserve Fund and the Guards Fund.●

2. The Army Reserve Fund appears, under the name of the ' Half-pay Fund,' to have been in existence sixty years ago. At that time, and until about the year 1826, the Commander-in-Chief carried to the credit of the fund portions of the sums paid for the purchase of commissions (where the selling officers were not entitled to receive the full amount) and occasionally the proceeds of first commissions ; the fund being applied, partly to make up the sums for which officers were allowed to sell on retiring from the army, and partly to the benefit of families of deserving officers.

3. The accounts of the Half-pay Fund, to the year 1820, signed by his Royal Highness the late Duke of York, are appended to the Report of the Commission on Army Purchase. The fund was carried on until the year 1856 ; and by the account signed by Messrs. Cox and Co., on the 11th July, the sum of £217 13s. 10d. stood to its credit. But about the year 1826, the sale of commissions for the benefit of the fund had ceased, and, subsequently to that date, the receipts and payments were comparatively small.

4. Meanwhile a new fund appears to have been created by the sale of half-pay commissions. At the death of the Duke of York in 1826, this fund was in credit to the extent of £80,000, and soon afterwards Lord Palmerston, who for a short time held the

services.

5. From 1841 to 1849, both the proceeds of half-pay commissions, and the differences previously paid into the 'Half-pay Fund,' appear to have been transferred to the paymaster-general, and applied to army services; but about the year 1850 the Reserve Fund was constituted on its present basis by the then Secretary at War. Since that time no balances have been paid over to any public account, and until 1860 no return in regard to the fund was rendered to Parliament. The present position of the fund may be gathered from the account for the year 1867, presented on the 13th February last. Including a balance from 1866 of £5,357, the total receipt for the year was £162,547 5s. The expenditure was £78,531 18s. 4d.; the balance, £84,015 6s. 8d., being invested in Exchequer Bills to the extent of £65,000.

6. The sources from which the fund is fed are:

(a) The sales, in certain cases, of commissions in succession to officers retiring on half-pay.

Formerly an officer retiring on half-pay was required to exchange with another, of the same rank, on the half-pay list; and no promotion resulted, unless the latter desired to sell, in which event the commissions in succession had always to be purchased. Under the regulations now in force, an officer of twenty-five years' full pay service is absolutely entitled to retire on half-pay, without bringing a half-pay officer back; the commissions in succession being sold for the benefit of the fund, except in cases where the retiring officer would probably have attained the rank of major-general within a period of two years, and where the officers next for promotion have, from long and distinguished service, claims for favourable consideration.

(b.) The differences between the purchasing price of certain commissions and the amounts which the sellers are entitled to receive.

The regulations provide (with unimportant modifications), that if an officer has not served for twenty years, he can only receive the value of any commission obtained by purchase, together with a sum of £50 for each year of home, and £100 for each year of foreign service, provided the whole amount does not exceed the regulation price of the commission he holds at the time he retires. The difference between the total sum payable to him, and that received from the purchasing officer, goes to the fund.

(c.) The differences between the values of full pay and half-pay commissions paid by officers who had received that amount on going to half-pay.

(d.) The sales, in certain cases, of first commissions.

First commissions are usually given by purchase, except in succession to vacancies caused by deaths, retirements on full pay, successions to the major-generals' establishment, and augmentations; but even in these cases they may be, and have been, sold. Thus, a considerable number of first commissions were sold for the benefit of the fund, on the augmentation of the Army in 1854.

7. The charges, borne by the fund, are of the following descriptions :—

(e.) Officers retiring on half-pay, whether from the line or the Ordnance corps, have been permitted to compound their half-pay, for a sum equivalent (in the case of an officer of the line) to the regulation price of the commission of the rank from which he retired, less the difference which he may have received between full and half-pay. These operations are called sales of half-pay commissions, but they are only permitted when there is a large balance on the reserve fund.

(f.) Cavalry officers, who entered previously to 1860, are entitled, on their retirement, to receive from the fund the difference between the old and new (regulation) prices of cavalry commissions. These differences are, in the case of a lieutenant-colonel, £1,675; of a major, £1,375; of a captain, £1,425; of a lieutenant, £490; and of a cornet, £390.

(g.) In 1861 the corps of Yeomen of the Guard, in 1862 that of Gentlemen-at-Arms, and in 1863 the Military Train, were respectively converted from purchase into non-purchase corps; 'compensations to existing interests' being granted out of the Reserve Fund.

(h.) Payments have also been made from the fund for the purpose of absorbing commissions which became super-, numerary, in consequence of reductions in the regimental establishments.

8. From returns laid before your Committee, it appears that the sale of commissions, in succession to officers retiring on half-pay, produced between the 1st April 1862 and the 31st December 1866, £338,678 ; and the differences between the sums received by retiring officers and those paid by the purchasers, £109,379 ; the total, £448,057, representing the sum received by the State, during less than six years, out of the purchase money paid by officers for their promotion in the army.

9. During the same period £204,881 was credited from the fund to cavalry officers purchasing their promotion; £46,625 was applied to the reform of the Corps of Yeomen of the Guard, Gentlemen-at-Arms, and the Military Train ; and £311,599 was paid, by way of composition of their half-pay, to half-pay officers of the Line, the Artillery, and the Engineers ; relieving the half-pay vote, but not to an amount equivalent to the composition.

10. The above charges were in excess of the receipts of the fund, and the balance has been mainly provided by the sale of first commissions.

11. From the above statements it will be evident that the receipts, and some of the payments of the fund, arise from regulations of much importance and nicety, forming links in the chain of the purchase system, which it will be impossible to deal with satisfactorily without entering upon the merits of that system. The reference to your Committee being limited to an enquiry into the origin, sources, and objects of the Reserve Funds, they are not prepared to give an opinion as to the extent to which commissions, in succession to retiring officers, should go with or without purchase; as to the restrictions, subject to which officers, who have obtained their commissions without purchase, should be permitted to sell ; or as to the system under which first commissions should be granted.

12. It is true that the recent regulation, entitling an officer, after 25 years' service, to retire, without bringing back another from half-pay, has had the effect of increasing the flow of promotion ; and the rule laid down by General Peel, when Secretary of State, under which any difference exceeding £450 between the regulation price paid to a retiring officer and that received from his successor, should be applied to the grant of a first commission without purchase, confers advantages on candidates for such commissions.

13. On the other hand, it cannot be disputed that if, to a greater extent than now, commissions, in succession to officers retiring on half-pay, were granted without purchase, advantages, at the expense of the fund, would result both to the retiring and the succeeding officers. From information received by your Committee, it appears that even under the recent modification of the regulations senior officers of different ranks have been unable to obtain their promotion without purchase in succession to retiring lieutenant-colonels, although their period of service was unusually long, and gave strong claims.

14. It appears, however, to your Committee that it is beyond the scope of their enquiry to take evidence as to the sufficiency of the present flow of promotion, whether by or without purchase ; or as to what proportion of first commissions should be sold.

15. But whatever opinion may be entertained as to the transactions which have been carried on by means of the fund, your Committee are of opinion that, in any case, the fund itself should be wound up.

16. Its existence has enabled the Secretary of State to levy, by his own authority, charges on persons seeking promotion or first appointment in the army, and to apply the proceeds to public objects, at his discretion. But no public monies should be at the disposal of a Minister, except such as are annually voted by Parliament, or charged on the Consolidated Fund ; and all sums received by public departments (unless otherwise applied by law) should be paid into the Exchequer.

17. Your Committee do not doubt that the reformation of the Corps of Yeomen of the Guard and Gentlemen-at-Arms, and of the Military Train, has been beneficial to the public service ; but that consideration does not appear to them sufficient to warrant the application to such purposes, without the authority of Parliament, of sums received from sales of commissions in other branches of the service. The same objection applies to the payments which have been made for the purchase of half-pay commissions in the Artillery and Engineers.

18. Your Committee accordingly recommend that all payments which may hereafter be made, for purposes now charged on the Reserve Fund, be defrayed from monies appropriated to such purposes by Parliament, and that any future receipts, together with the balance at the credit of the Fund, be paid into the Exchequer. Among these receipts would be included the pur-

chase money of a commission, where the seller is not entitled to receive the whole; but in this case the net amount only would be payable to the Exchequer.

19. Your Committee are also of opinion that any regulations for the composition of half-pay should only be made under the authority of a statute. They would refer to the proceedings, in 1867, of the Select Committee on Retirement from the Non-Purchase Corps, in evidence of the difficulties attending this question.

20. Your Committee have not deemed it necessary to take evidence as to the Guards' Fund. The receipts and expenditure of that fund are given in the Appendix to the Report of the Select Committee on Military Reserve Funds of 1867; and there appears to be no reason why the former should not be paid into the Exchequer, and the latter charged on Votes of Parliament.

APPENDIX II.

[See p. 60.]

423. MARRIAGES TO BE DISCOURAGED.—Commanding officers of regiments, who have ample experience of the very great inconvenience arising to the service, and to the public, from the improvident marriage of soldiers, are to discountenance such connexions, and to explain to the men that their comforts, as soldiers, are in a very small degree increased by their marriage, while the inconvenience and distress naturally accruing therefrom are serious and unavoidable, particularly when regiments are ordered to embark for foreign service.

424. CONSENT OF COMMANDING OFFICER.—Every soldier, previously to his marriage, should obtain the consent of his commanding officer, and state the name and condition of the woman he proposes to marry, and whether she be a spinster or a widow. In granting their consent commanding officers should most carefully consider the claims of the soldier, as regards good conduct and length of service, and when deserving soldiers cannot be admitted on the strength of their corps as married men, their applications should be registered, with a view to their wives being taken on the strength as vacancies occur.

425. Vacancies abroad; how filled.—Officers commanding regiments on foreign stations are to specify in the returns which they transmit to the depôt companies at home, the vacancies which occur in the regulated number of soldiers' wives, and are to name those whom they may recommend to be sent out to fill such vacancies. Soldiers' wives who have joined the regiment without authority, or who may, by the permission of the Commander-in-Chief (obtained through the Quartermaster-General), accompany officers as servants in their families, and afterwards quit such service, are not to benefit by being allowed at any future time to fill vacancies on the establishment of soldiers' wives, which vacancies must be reserved for those who have waited at home for their turn to go out.

426. Sleeping out of quarters.—No soldiers are to be allowed to sleep out of their quarters permanently, except those who are borne on the strength of their corps as married men, or who are married with leave, and together with their wives are of good character. Married men who are allowed to mess and sleep out of barracks for their own comfort and the benefit of their families, must be regular in attending to their duties, orderly in their lodgings or quarters, exact in their dress, and never leave their lodgings or quarters after tattoo except when on duty or on leave. Any man not obeying these orders is to be immediately brought into barracks.

427. Men married without leave.—In cases where a soldier married without leave has any children, the commanding officer may use his discretion in granting permission to the man to be out of the troop, battery, or company mess, in order to support his family.

APPENDIX III.

[See p. 50.]

Most of the Regiments took the county denominations which they now bear in consequence of a Royal order, dated 31st August 1772, directing them to take the titles of certain counties, so that in each case a connection and mutual attachment between the corps and that county should be cultivated, in order to promote the success of the recruiting service. Of the 109 infantry regiments of the line, besides the Rifle brigade, 87 are attached to counties, blishment. The unattached regiments should be connected with districts with which regiments are not now associated. For instance, Lancashire, possessing a population of 1,190,480, has only one regiment attached to it. The different cavalry regiments should in like manner be connected with the Yeomanry Cavalry and the Light Horse and Mounted Rifle Volunteers (two or three local corps to each cavalry regiment); the Royal Artillery should be associated, for giving instruction and receiving recruits, with the powerful militia and Volunteer Artillery force; and the Royal Engineers with the Engineer Volunteers. All officers of local corps should receive their commissions upon condition of passing through a short prescribed course of instruction with the regular corps with which they are affiliated; or, in the case of the Yeomanry and Volunteer Cavalry, in a cavalry school which will probably be established in connection with the Military College.

The Recruiting Commissioners of 1867 report 'Strong evidence has been laid before us, showing the advantages resulting to recruiting from a local connection being maintained between individual corps and certain localities. Men enlist much more freely in corps which already contain a number of their friends and acquaintances, and such connections should therefore, we consider, be in every way encouraged. Much may be done in this direction, by strengthening the relations that exist between particular corps of the Army and particular Militia Regiments, whether arising from County denominations or other circumstances; and the object might also be facilitated by the Line Regiments supplying good non-commissioned officers to the corresponding Militia Regiments, and by directing the volunteering from each regiment to one, or even two or three Regiments of the Line.'

Illustrations of the advantage of local connections in recruiting may be found in the practice of the Guards, of the Royal Artillery before their recruiting was made general, and of particular regiments of the line; but the most remarkable instance is the connection of the Royal Marines with Devonshire, where the name of this corps is a household word, and service in the Marines is so popular that there is a choice of recruits, and strict enquiries are made into character.

Circumstances have so changed since the date of the following memorandum, by the Adjutant-General, Sir Harry Calvert, that an exact comparison can no longer with advantage be made; but his plan and mine are based upon the same principles, and the objects he desired to attain have been provided for by me in a manner suited to the present time. The most important diffe-- rence is that, while the scheme of 1809 is partly based upon the ballot, which is only another name for conscription, that of 1868 depends entirely upon voluntary service.

Plan for Improving the Military Force of the Country.

Horse Guards,
February 6th, 1809.

I would propose that every Regiment of the Line, with the exception of the 60th, should be composed of two battalions.

The first battalion should, according to its effective strength, be on the establishment of 800, 1,000, or 1,200, and should, as at present, be engaged for unlimited service, in regard to time and place. This, if the plan succeeded, as I feel confident it would, gives on an average a disposable force of 100,000 men.

The second battalion should be uniformly of the establishment of 1,000, composed by men obtained by ballot, as the present Militia, but officered by officers of the Regular service, forming, in every respect, an integral part of the Regiment, passing in their turn, according to rank, into the first battalion.

The services of the men of the second battalions, in considera- tion of their being raised by ballot, must be limited to Great Britain and Ireland, and the Islands in the Channel: this would give us a force for home defence of rather more than 100,000 men— a number, it is to be observed, inferior to that which was raised for the Militia service during the late war, but possessing this marked superiority over the present Militia, that it would be commanded by officers of the Army, whose habits and feelings would naturally introduce among their men a predilection for the Regular service, and that its services would be equally applicable to Ireland as to Britain.

I would recommend that the ten Royal Veteran Battalions should be retained, with the power of placing such of their officers as may, from time to time, become, through age and infirmities, unfit for duty, on a retired pay, becoming their respective ranks, and referring to their best years devoted to their country. Without some such arrangement, it is evident, from the nature of things, these respectable and highly useful corps must become inefficient.

I would place all the rest of the force of the country in Local Militia, Yeomanry Cavalry, and Volunteer corps, the latter composed of officers and men who are willing to enrol themselves in corps of not less than 600, under engagements to subject themselves to such drills as may be deemed necessary to fit them to act with Regular troops, to serve, in case of emergency, in any part of Great Britain, and to support themselves entirely at their own expense (arms excepted), till called out on permanent duty, when they should receive military pay, and be in every respect amenable to martial law.

No officer of the two latter descriptions of force should receive a higher rank than that of lieutenant-colonel commandant.

The Local Militia to be formed upon the same military principle as the other parts of the Army. The numbers of the battalions must depend on the extent and population of the counties to which they belong; but the strength of the companies and the establishment of the battalions should, as far as circumstances will permit, be equalised. The whole, or any part, should be liable to be called out according to the exigency of the service; but by this arrangement their duties would become comparatively so little burdensome, that it might be presumed the commissions would be held by gentlemen of the first respectability in their respective counties.

The amount of the force produced by this plan is as follows :—

Regular Infantry of the Line for general service
   exclusive of Regular Cavalry, Foot Guards
   and Veteran Battalions, and the six battalions
   of the 60th Regiment* 100,000
Second battalions, balloted men, with officers of
   the line, for service limited to Great Britain
   and Ireland 100,000
Local Militia, at least   200,000
Volunteer Cavalry 32,000
Volunteer corps, on a principle calculated to
   render them really effective for general
   service, probably not less than .   .   . 100,000

The result would prove, I conclude, as follows :—The Militia becomes what it ought constitutionally to be—the basis of our

* This refers only to the numbered regiments. The West India regiments, the garrison battalions, the foreign and provisional corps, are not included in this computation.

national force. The Local Militia assumes the uniform, colours, and every other article of equipment of the Regiment of the Line belonging to its county. In short, it adopts the County Regiment as part of itself, and gives every encouragement to its men to enlist into this corps. Let the men of the second battalion receive the same encouragement to extend their services into the first battalion, and their places be immediately supplied by volunteers at a low bounty from the Local Militia. I say, by volunteers, because I do not believe there would be found any difficulty in filling up these vacancies; but if, contrary to expectation, there should be any, a ballot must be resorted to, because the very essence of the plan I venture to submit for consideration is the absolute certainty of the second battalions being kept complete as long as their services are required; and I humbly conceive that a very little arrangement would be necessary to insure a large proportion of the men repairing to their colours, in the event of any sudden emergency calling for their services, at times when they might not be embodied.

If I see the subject right, this would establish what has yet been unsuccessfully attempted—a real and useful connection between the different branches of the military force of the country, and by these means actually connect the Regiment of the Line with the county whose name it bears.

It would, by these means, present the fairest prospect of placing the recruiting of regiments on the most certain and respectable footing, without at all preventing their employing the means now in practice, if they found it desirable. My opinion of the eligibility of this, or of some plan of the same nature, has been long formed; and the experience of each year more and more convinces me that every measure adopted for the increase of our military force, which does not place it on an *assured* and *permanent* footing, is illusory and inadequate to the object. After the long and repeated warnings we have had, it will be most unpardonable, if we are not prepared to repel the attack of our enemy, by efforts commensurate with the difficulties and dangers with which we are threatened, and the importance of the objects for which we contend.

LONDON: PRINTED BY
SPOTTISWOODE AND CO., NEW-STREET SQUARE

CPSIA information can be obtained
at www.ICGtesting.com
Printed in the USA
BVHW04*1046170918
527708BV00015B/1920/P